Conquering The Front Line Leadership Quest

CHRIS MIFSUD

Copyright © 2016 Chris Mifsud
All rights reserved.

ISBN: 1537774689
ISBN 13: 9781537774688

PREFACE

Conquering the Frontline Leadership quest is no easy task but it's not an impossible one either, from all Leadership levels being a Frontline Leader is the toughest, you need to bring a group of individuals and turn them in to a unified team, by getting their buy in for the Company's vision and mission and lead them with empathy.

I worked in the business world when Leadership was called a 'Manager' or 'Boss'.

In those days on reflection were very easy to manage people who worked for you, it was a time of my way or the highway.

If I say jump you say how high, that style of Leadership was so antiquated it was based on fear, or forcing people to do what you want without being questioned.

If they do not like it, they know where the door is sort of reply from the boss.

Those of my age can remember what it was like, those of a younger age are lucky not to have experienced it.

Thankfully for change we find ourselves in a totally different environment, the business world has transformed and came to realize the greatest asset they have is their people.

They invest a lot in their people and the Leaders they appoint.

I have seen many Leaders operate and have to say there is no one size fits all, different people lead in different ways however there are some fundamentals that all Leaders need to follow for their success.

I will share some of these fundamentals with you, however please remember there are more, so do not look at this as, I read it now, and therefore, I am a great Leader. It takes practice to become a great basketball player, a gold medalist, a great leader.

I am not showing how to re-invent the wheel but just remind you that it is there and you should use it.

A Great Leader does the following:

>   *L*earns
>   *E*mpowers
>   *A*ppreciates
>   *D*evelops
>   *E*ngages
>   *R*espects

LEARNS

Leaders grow by learning and great Leaders never stop learning, so what should Leaders learn about?

That is very simple to answer, they learn about the people in their team, why is this important you might ask?

Well let me give you an example; remember the last time you were invited to a stranger's home?

You arrive knock on the door they greet you and ask you to come in, you oblige being slightly nervous and stand till they ask you to have a seat and then they ask you if you would like something to drink.

Now remember the last time you went to a friend's house, you arrive knock on the door, the door opens and you say 'hey how is it going'? (or something to that effect) Immediately you just waltz in have a seat and in some cases you just go to the kitchen and get yourself something to drink.

You see what I mean?

You are more comfortable with people you know. Of course the people you know now remember the first time you met them?

They were like the stranger you would meet today for the first time. So what changed?

Well you got to know them and after a while you became comfortable around them to share with them your thoughts and how you feel.

Now, do you see why getting to know your people is important?

Sure your colleagues at work are not going to share with you their deepest darkest secrets with you however the more you get to know them the closer you get, the more they tend to trust you.

This in turn makes them more open to speak with you when they have concerns, when they are not happy etc.

Getting to know your people will make your work easier.

Do not make the mistake of saying, great, now I know my people so if they ever need something they can come and find me in my little corner.

It does not work that way, you still need to be aware of what is going on, I can assure you there is no way you will ever know everything about people, it is a constant learning process.

I recommend to hold One to One meetings with your people

The frequency is up to you and depends on how many people you have in your team.

In any case please do have One to One meetings, these are the greatest source of learning about your people, also please ensure that you do not turn it in a performance review.

Have a conversation with each individual, ask them how their weekend was, find out what are their hobbies, if they like sports etc.

I found this works even better by leaving the office and going for a coffee nearby.

So if you are not doing One to One's start now and set yourself a target.

Find three new things that you do not know already from each person, once you know, then your conversations can be tailored around their interest the next time you have another.

Please do not just wait till your next One to One to learn about your people you can still do this by simply talking with them during the working day.

Learning about your people is very important to you and your team's success.

Listen to your team members' opinions, any suggestions they might have, do not be afraid to share your ideas with the team.

Give them the sense of belonging and importance they all deserve.

This is so powerful to be able to walk up one raining cold morning to one of your team members who shared with you how much they love sunny weather to acknowledge to them you share their dissatisfaction and hope for a brighter day.

Of course this is just a simple example but I hope you manage to understand my meaning and how powerful it is for your team's camaraderie.

There are other things Leaders should learn which are important, such as how to better communicate with their people.

*As the saying goes, **it's not what you say, it's how you say it**, this should never be underestimated.*

Learning about your people's strengths and areas of improvement (I did not use the word weakness on purpose) again a perfect example of how to say it.

Learning how to set goals for your people, you might say 'oh that is easy', but it is not as easy as just giving them targets you want to achieve.

It is important to give them realistic goals that would stretch them but are within the realm of possibility to achieve.

If you come up to me and tell me that my goal is to climb Mount Everest in 5 hours, I would lose complete confidence in your ability to be a Leader as you have no clue about my strengths, let alone my areas of improvement.

There are many more areas Leaders need to improve by learning, however for this particular session take on board learning about your people and do the following:

Promise yourself on your <u>next One to One meeting find out 3 new things that you do not know about your people</u> and use them in your conversations with them.

Remember also that great leaders are avid learners themselves.

They are willing to listen and learn from others to grow their own leadership skills.

EMPOWER

'Leaders empower their people, definition of empower is permits, allows, inspires, encourages and energizes'.

Permit your people to show you what they know, we all like to be proud of what we know and do.

Get them out of their comfort zone, let them know you have faith in them and trust them with additional tasks, allow them to make mistakes and let them know.

It is ok to make mistakes as long as they learn from them.

If your people are afraid of making mistakes they will not be empowered to try anything new for fear of making mistakes.

All great Leaders have made mistakes and or failed on their way to the top, so why should it not apply to your people or you for that matter.

Help them learn to make their own decisions.

The next time one of your people approaches you with a question or decision to be made, do not make it for them or just give them the answer.

Ask them questions give them suggestions; ask them to weigh the repercussions of making a decision.

Help them see the whole picture but let them come up with the answer.

I have always used this as a tool to empower them and give them the satisfaction of their ability to be part of something more than just an employee doing his standard job they were hired for, it gives them a greater sense of purpose in the workplace.

If you have ambitious people in your team embrace them.

You will know who they are, they are the ones that always want to do more, do better.

If you have these people, ensure you delegate tasks to them and trust them to get the job done.

Do not feel threatened by them, do not fear them but embrace them as valuable members in your team, treated properly they will help you with the rest of the team in achieving great results.

I remember once I was in a meeting with other Leaders and we were discussing the kind of people we need to hire.

I was advocating I like to hire ambitious people with strong characters.

One Leader came up to me and professed he will not hire these kind of people as he was worried they would take his job.

This is true and yes there are Leaders out there that are insecure and fear someone in their team will be a threat and steal their job.

These people should not be in Leadership roles - they do a great disservice to the Company they represent.

Then there are some who are just afraid to let go for fear of losing control.

This is a real handicap to their growth, they seem to want to be in control of everything their team does.

They are often afraid to delegate, believing they are the best person to do the job believing it is easier and quicker if they do it themselves.

All this will only create additional work for them and coupled with their actual job of leading their people will lead them to very stressful times.

These Leaders are doing a great injustice to their employees.

They are sending out the signal that they are not trusted to get the job done or done well.

How could these Leaders expect to have the trust of their people if they are showing lack of trust in them?

They are also stunting the growth of their people by micro managing what they do. This will not allow them to expand their knowledge beyond the basics they have been through when they first started.

You have to ask, where is their development going to come from?

Where is their ability to make decisions going to come from?

What about their ability to make mistakes, when is that going to be able to happen so they can learn from them?

Great Leaders first hire the right people to ensure they can trust them with tasks which would be more complex than their basic learning.

This in turn will allow their employees to have the confidence of their Leaders to trust them.

Confidence is a great thing to have, it helps tackle the ever coming challenges we face in our role on a daily basis.

By letting go - Leaders are helping their people grow and be experts in their role, this way Leaders will have the time to focus on their people's development.

This is a key component to having a great team and a succession plan, a key part of success has been very wisely stated many times in the past. I will use the quote here to illustrate the meaning of this chapter in just one sentence.

> *"I surround myself with people who I believe are better than me in their specific areas of expertise, and then I get out of their way, delegate to them and try to give them as much support as possible."*

So remember that no one person can do it all alone, <u>empower</u> your people and they will reach their potential and through your great Leadership achieve your goals.

APPRECIATES

Leaders need to show appreciation towards their people.

They need to let them know "we are all in it together" there are many occasions on a daily basis to show appreciation to your people.

When you see a team member helping their colleagues show how much you appreciate it, say thank you to that person, doing so will make them feel better, feel motivated by knowing their leader saw and appreciated what they did.

Appreciation does not cost you anything to give, you should do it as often as you can, please make sure it is sincere and honest, your people will see right through insincerity.

Praise good work done and make sure that you do it in public in front of the rest of the team.

Showing appreciation also shows the team you care about what they do and the efforts they are putting in their work.

It also lets them know you are aware of what is going on in the team.

Use rewards and create friendly competitions for them, make it fun - recognition is part of showing appreciation,

Some might be saying why should I bother?

They are paid for their job, is it not enough?

No, that is the wrong way of thinking and I repeat again it is something that will cost you nothing and has so much value.

Is it not nice you can give something that cost absolutely zero yet you get so much in return?

By doing this you foster loyalty and eagerness from the team to do that little extra and all this without having to force anyone to do it.

As a reminder let's go back to our childhood, as kids we always liked praise and appreciation from our parents.

When we got good results in school, decided to clean our room etc.

Praise stays with us like a beacon of person pride and sincere honest appreciation always makes us feel good and worthy.

Another quick powerful thing you can start doing if you are not already, is make sure you know everyone's Birthday and gather the team to congratulate and celebrate the individual's Birthday.

Once you start doing this you will be amazed how you will even have the team whipping around to get a present for that person, hence now you have the whole team getting involved and become closer to each other.

If you, like many others hold a weekly team meeting, why not get some cookies or fruit for everyone during the meeting?

Also encourage them to air their views in the meeting by letting them know you are interested and appreciate their opinion.

Remember people leave for different reasons but one of them is they are not appreciated by their leaders, so ensure you invest that little bit to keep them with you.

DEVELOPS

Leaders need to have a good development plan for their team.

How do we do this?

Well we need to know the interest of the individual, which path they would like to follow and grow in the company.

Remember not everyone wants to become a Leader, developing people does not only consist of someone wanting to become a Leader.

Some might like to take the technical path, project path etc.

Leaders need to ask their people what is their interest and once it is identified ensure they will get the training necessary to start their development.

Please do not make the common mistake of thinking once you identified their development need and send them for the training your job is done.

It is not and it is very far from it.

Follow closely what they are learning in the training and ask them if they are finding it valuable and are happy that they are receiving this training.

This you can do during your One to One meetings with them, once the training is done then your job really begins, you need to ensure you will find projects for them to be involved in to be able to practice what they have learned in training.

This is where development happens and not in the classroom during the training period.

Let's take one simple example for better understanding.

Let's imagine you had a team member who wanted to learn how to present Power Point Presentations.

You agreed to send them to the training being given by the Company's training department.

Great that is just the first step, after that the learning and development will start:

You have a meeting with Senior Leadership and need to present how your team is doing, what challenges you are facing what were your successes so far, your results etc. this usually requires a PPT presentation right?

Usually yes.

What should you do?

Why not assign the PPT preparation to the team member who just had the training and wants to develop this skillset?

Exactly what you need to do, this in turn will help that person develop and practice what they learned in training.

Remember practice makes perfect they say.

Follow the above process with all your team members and you will be on your way to giving real development.

Your team's development is very crucial in order to retain them.

People need to see that they are not going to get stuck in the same position forever.

Developing them will ensure that they will have the opportunity to grow and follow their ambitions.

Some Leaders don't like to do this because they are selfish or insecure.
However, unless they would like to lose their team members, they need to get used to this fact and accept it, as a Leader.
I am sure you have your own ambition to grow.
I am sure you do not want to stay in the same job for the rest of your career...
How would you feel if your Leader does not give you the opportunity to grow?
I am sure you would not like it.
Development is part of succession planning.
Before you can move forward you need to ensure you are developing your own replacement, if you don't it will be difficult for your Company to promote you.
Identify your most talented people who have the interest to become Leaders and help develop them as mentioned above.
Leadership development is of course not as easy as developing someone in preparing Power Point Presentations, it is more complex.
You will need to help develop their Leadership skills.

(This book might help as a handbook, one that you might pass on to your future leaders)
Utilize your experience in your position to mentor them and coach them, delegate to them.
When you are going on vacation, put one of them as your replacement and let them lead the team in your absence.

Upon your return get their feedback on' how they feel they did' and what they learned, speak to the team members and get their feedback on how it was in your absence.

Of course you do not need to wait until you go on vacation to develop your successor, you can do it on a daily basis.

Give them exposure to problem solving, decision making, and how to engage the team members, of course, there will be certain situations you will not be able to get them involved in, but in most cases they can learn from how you deal with the situations that arise in the team.

It is common knowledge and understanding that each individual is responsible for their own development.

When a team member tells me they would like to develop themselves I will do something about it.

In many ways that is true however I urge you to encourage your team members to want to develop their potential, this will help you show them that you have their best interest at heart.

Do not try to force them to develop, it won't work.

Why?

As the saying goes, **"You can lead a horse to water but you can't make it drink."**

As a Leader you also still need to develop if you want to go to the next level and I am sure you do.

You have the responsibility to approach your Leader and request your development areas are fulfilled.

If you have a good Leader their interest would be to get you developed since they have their ambition to move to the next level too.

If you do not have a good Leader you need to ensure you get the development you need to be able to continue on your path to growth.

Seek mentoring and coaching from your Leader or other senior leaders in the organization they will help you continue grow in your career, read Leadership books, take Leadership courses.

Remember that you should not just learn something and just stick to it, you need to expand on what you learn, put it to practice, it is the only way to evolve.

So make sure you develop yourself and as importantly develop those you lead and have a good succession plan.

ENGAGES

Leaders need firstly to be engaged themselves and more importantly need their team to be engaged.

Without this there is not success.

Is it really that important for the success of a business?

Of course it is, without Engagement of the employees a business will not have much success.

After all, a Company is only Bricks and Mortar or simply put 'a name'.

However, what makes that Company and what drives it is very simple; it's People.

A Company succeeds or fails by the actions of its People, that is why Engagement of its people is paramount.

Is there a magic pill we can give everyone so they are engaged?

Is there a one size fit all program to get everyone Engaged?

The answer is simple, NO.

The main reason is that the one thing people have in common is that they are all unique.

We have to work at it from the top person all the way down to the general population in the Company.

Leaders have a very important role to play when it comes to Engagement at work, it is part of their fundamental role to do so.

If Leaders are not engaged how do you expect them to have their teams Engaged?

The first thing that needs to be done is ensure Leaders are engaged.

Once you have that you are on the road to success.

However, only after a lot of work being invested.

You will need is commitment from your team members.

They need to be committed to the cause.

They want, thirst for and need pride in what they do to feel they are important.

They want to feel that the role they have is an important part of the building blocks in achieving success.

Make sure that your team members are doing a job they like.

If they do not like what they are doing, they will not be engaged.

What was pointed out in this book earlier, regarding empowering, appreciation and developing are important to get your team engaged.

Engagement is not a stand-alone module of success.

For engagement to work you really need every individual to be engaged.

You cannot think by having 9 out of 10 engaged you are doing a great job, everyone in your team needs to be engaged.

As an example think of a chain, it is made out of links which are connected together.

If they are all strong, you can see the strength of that chain, however if one of those links is not as strong as the other what would you think will happen to that chain?

It will break, as the saying goes **'A chain is only as strong as its weakest link'** *- and that is why you need the whole team fully engaged.*

Another example, imagine you are leading a Soccer team, you put 11 players on that pitch all 11 are great in their role, now you see that you have 10 players are really engaged and performing to the highest level.

They are working in harmony covering for each other if one makes mistakes, yet you have the goalkeeper sitting on the ground reading a book, do you think you can win that game?

I don't think so.

Is having an engaged team easy?

Absolutely not.

Is it impossible?

Absolutely not.

It takes constant work, you are dealing with people, not machines.

You cannot set people up to be engaged and just flip a switch, they are unique individuals.

Some wake up happy in the morning and merrily go to work and are able to self-engage themselves.

Others might come to work in a bad mood for whatever reason.

Leaders need to notice these things, they are very important for the success of your team to be engaged.

In a nutshell your team members need to feel valued, involved, appreciated and important.

This is done by the Leader showing them that they all play an important part in the team.

*Instill the **'All for one and one for all philosophy'**, let them know your success and their success can only be achieved when all are engaged and working towards a common goal.*

When goals are reached celebrate success with the team let them know it was only possible to achieve thanks to their contribution, remember the example of the Chain and the Soccer team.

Engagement is one of the things that Companies can successfully assess, most companies organize Employee Engagement Surveys, some do it monthly, quarterly, half yearly or yearly.

As a Leader you should use this to gauge your success in engaging your team member.

Encourage your team to participate in these surveys.

Some Leaders think they have a great result if they have 100% engagement.

That of course is a correct assumption unless you have 60% participation rate, then you have a lot of work to do since you have 40% who could not be bothered to be engaged enough to participate.

This is why your priority is to have 100% participation rate that means your team are engaged enough to give their feedback.

I would rather have 100% participation and 90% positive result, this way I know that I am only 10% away from perfection.

By the way having 90% engagement for your whole team is a fantastic result, 100% is not that common or easy to achieve but you should have that as your target.

With the previous scenario of 60% participation rate and 100% positive result I am 40% away from achieving my goal of 100% engagement.

Tell all your team members that you really want them to participate and be brutally honest in their responses.

Remind them that these surveys are anonymous and their honest feedback will only help you improve where things are lacking.

Do not try to tell them to fill the surveys in by writing down that all is fantastic, you should not influence their feedback just ensure they participate.

If your Company does not have engagement measuring surveys it would be worth you creating one yourself for your team.

The reason is you would need to gauge how your team is doing.

Are they happy at the workplace?

Do they feel they are contributing?

Do they feel their opinion matters?

Are they appreciated?

As a leader it is in your interest to know these things so you will be able to retain your employees.

RESPECT

Leaders need to fundamentally understand trying everything highlighted in this book will be useless unless they have the respect of their team members.

Yes.

Respect is the most fundamental asset you will need to earn in order lead.

Let us amplify this point.

Respect cannot be demanded it has to be earned.

You need to work for it by being genuine, true to your belief and always doing what you say you will do.

This of course is not a one-way street, by the same token your team members need to earn your respect.

It's a mutual thing.

Respect leads to trust.

People will listen to what a respected person has to say.

Try to demand respect and you will get it only shown to your face but behind your back it would be a different story.

Respecting others should not be hard to do since we all want to be respected as human beings, so how do you earn respect?

Well firstly by being open to other people's opinions.

Whenever any of your team members expresses an idea, take the time to listen and engage in the conversation in a polite manner even if you do not agree with the idea itself.

If any of your team members make a mistake, do not admonish them in front of their peers, ask them to join you for a meeting and discuss with them the situation in private.

By correcting a team member in front of their peers will only achieve embarrassment to the individual which goes totally the opposite direction of what you want to achieve with your team.

Do not be tempted to share your opinion about a particular team member's failing with another team member especially behind that persons back.

Many people fall in this trap and it is a very dangerous slippery slope to losing respect of your team, even from the person that you are confiding in.

Why?

Because that person will be thinking what does my Leader say to others behind my back.

Respect takes time to earn, however it will take only one instance to lose it and it would be much harder to build it back to the level you had it.

Remember that you are part of your team if your team is succeeding or not and as such, you must take responsibility for their actions.

Great Leaders always accept responsibility of their team performance and always give praise to the team.

If you would like to lose respect of your team instantly just make sure you take credit for their success and give them the blame for the failures.

Respected Leaders know that being Leaders is an honor.

They realize that their role as a leader is not some privilege to impose their idea of autocratic rule.

You have been entrusted to lead people, do it with respect and care.

Never look at your team as a bunch of people who are beneath you and are there to just do what you want with them.

As I said in the beginning of this book, I worked in a time were bosses demanded respect, did not bother to earn it, they felt they have been given some special power to do as they pleased.

Those days thankfully are far gone, we are at an age of knowing that to get the best results you need to respect and be respected the earned way not demanded.

Imagine for one moment that you decided to disrespect one of your team members by shouting at them in front of their colleagues because they did a mistake.

They may have ignored what you asked or you did not like that they violated the dress code one particular day.

What would you have achieved?

Well, you might think that you achieved showing your power, you might believe that it won't happen again.

Well I have to disagree; it could still happen again.

Now what did you lose?

Well for starters you managed to embarrass the individual.

I do not think you would like to be embarrassed by your Leader either, that embarrassment will lead to resentment by the individual even though he was wrong.

You would create a group within your team that will sympathize with their colleague who in turn will resent what you did for the simple fact that if you did it to that individual you can do it to others.

Result?

Loss of respect.

Being a Leader is not an easy task especially as a front line Leader, you have to walk that very fine line of giving the Company the results it needs to move forward and at the same time deal with your people in a way to achieve those results.

Also remember that there is a difference between being liked by your team and being respected.

Just because your team like you it does not mean they respect you.

For example, they would like you if you let them do whatever they wanted, such as come to work late, leave early, have a lot of breaks and you don't mind if they are not doing their fair share of work.

Believe me if you let them do all these things they would definitely like you.

Remember your job is not to be liked, but to be respected and trusted.

Your team follows your Leadership for these two things and not because they like you.

Being liked is an added bonus, if it is for the right reasons.

I hope you found this a good read and is able to help you better understand your role as a Leader, what is mentioned here is the basics we need to constantly remember to becoming great not just as Leaders but also as unique individual human beings.

Do not look at this as everything you need to learn or do to be a Leader, you need to build on what you read here, use your mind to expand your knowledge of dealing with people.

www.ingramcontent.com/pod-product-compliance
Lightning Source LLC
Chambersburg PA
CBHW070302190526
45169CB00004B/1503